Personal Branding for Developers

Build Your Portfolio, Grow Your Network, and Stand Out in Tech

Taylor Royce

Copyright © 2024 Taylor Royce

All rights reserved.

DEDICATION

I hope this book gives all developers navigating the always changing digital landscape the confidence to embrace their individual journeys and create a distinctive brand that embodies their knowledge and enthusiasm. We are all inspired by your commitment to development and innovation.

CONTENTS

ACKNOWLEDGMENTS 1

CHAPTER 1 1

Developers' Understanding of Personal Branding 1

    1.1. Personal branding: what is it? 1

    1.2. The Value of a Powerful Brand in Technology 4

    1.3. Typical Myths Regarding Personal Branding 7

CHAPTER 2 11

Establishing Your Own Developer Persona 11

    2.1. Determining Your Fundamental Abilities and Advantages 11

    2.2. Branding: Personal vs. Professional Identity 14

    2.3 Making a Personal Mission Statement 17

CHAPTER 3 22

Creating a Recurring Message and Theme 22

    3.1 Selecting a Uniform Visual Identity 22

    3.2. Establishing a Harmonious Voice and Tone 26

    3.3 Aligning Your Online and Offline Presence 30

CHAPTER 4 35

Putting Together a Strong Portfolio 35

    4.1 Important Components of a Developer Portfolio 35

    4.2. Highlighting Your Contributions and Projects 40

    4.3. Resources and Systems for Developing Your Portfolio 44

CHAPTER 5 50

Producing Content That Shows Off Your Knowledge 50

5.1. Blogging: Exchanging Experiences and Knowledge.....................50

5.2. Making Use of Video Tutorials and YouTube............................. 56

5.3. Participating in Forums and Industry Discussions........................61

CHAPTER 6..68

Building a Powerful Social Media Presence..68

6.1. Selecting Appropriate Social Media Channels.............................. 68

6.2. Methods for Developing an Active Audience............................... 74

6.3. Using GitHub, Twitter, and LinkedIn to Manage Your Personal Brand..78

CHAPTER 7..84

Establishing Professional Connections and Networking.......................84

7.1. The Developer Community's Use of Networking..........................84

7.2. Participating in Industry Gatherings and Conferences................... 87

7.3. Working Together with Other Programmers.................................90

CHAPTER 8..94

Participating in Community and Open-Source Initiatives.....................94

8.1. Advantages of Contributions to Open-Source............................... 94

8.2. Locating Initiatives to Participate in...97

8.3. Presenting Your Work in Open Source.. 100

CHAPTER 9..104

Establishing Yourself as an Authority in Your Field............................104

9.1. Establishing Your Authority... 104

9.2 Presentations and Public Speaking at Events................................107

9.3. Composing White Papers and Technical Articles........................110

CHAPTER 10..114

Keeping Your Personal Brand Strong and Developing It 114

10.1. Changing to Fit New Technologies with Your Brand 114

10.2: Handling Online Reviews and Your Reputation 117

10.3. Long-Term Methods for Developing Your Personal Brand 120

ABOUT THE AUTHOR 124

ACKNOWLEDGMENTS

Please accept my sincere gratitude to all those who helped to make this book possible. I want to start by expressing my gratitude to my family and friends for their constant encouragement and support along this journey. I was inspired to write because of your faith in my idea.

I want to express my gratitude to my IT sector mentors and colleagues who have offered their knowledge and experiences, which has improved my comprehension of personal branding in the developer community. Your advice has been really helpful.

My writing has been influenced and enlightened by the work of innumerable authors and thought leaders, for which I am especially grateful. Your commitment to information sharing has greatly influenced how I approach this topic.

Finally, I want to thank all of the people who have read this book. What motivates me to share this knowledge is your ambition to develop, learn, and make a name for yourself in the digital industry. I believe this book will be a useful tool for you as you develop your unique brand. I appreciate you coming along on this journey with me!

CHAPTER 1

DEVELOPERS' UNDERSTANDING OF PERSONAL BRANDING

Personal branding has become crucial for developers who want to stand out and progress in the cutthroat IT industry of today. Beyond technical proficiency, the capacity to promote oneself and communicate a distinct identity can significantly improve prospects for employment, teamwork, and thought leadership. The definition of personal branding, its significance in the IT industry, and typical misunderstandings developers have about creating a personal brand will all be covered in this chapter.

1.1. Personal branding: what is it?

The process of purposefully establishing and showcasing a person's distinct set of abilities, experiences, values, and reputation to the outside world is known as personal branding. For developers, it entails demonstrating not just technical proficiency but also their problem-solving methodology, enthusiasm for particular technologies, and interactions with the larger tech community.

The brand of a developer communicates:

- **Skill and Area of Expertise:** Regardless of whether you are a full-stack, frontend, or backend developer, your brand should clearly state your main areas of expertise.

- **Work Ethic and Values:** How you tackle problems, your dedication to lifelong learning, and the values that direct your work.

- **Personality and Communication Style:** How you interact with people, whether in professional conversations, blog entries, or social media. This humanizes your knowledge and increases your relatability.

Creating a professional story that is valuable, genuine, and consistent is the goal of building a personal brand; it goes beyond simply promoting oneself. A strong personal brand helps build credibility and trust in the IT community by intentionally influencing how people see you.

Developers can accomplish this in a number of ways:

- **Technical Blogs:** Writing about technology, tools, or projects that you are enthusiastic about.

- **Contributions that are open-source:** Sharing your code on websites like GitHub lets peers and possible employers view your work.

Engaging with the community and establishing oneself as a thought leader are two benefits of speaking at conferences or meetups.

Social Media Presence: Taking part in tech-related conversations on sites like LinkedIn, Twitter, or even developer-only forums like Stack Overflow.

The process of developing your personal brand is continuous and changes as your profession does. When done correctly, it yields significant benefits but necessitates consistency and honesty.

1.2. The Value of a Powerful Brand in Technology

A strong personal brand can lead to many opportunities in the tech sector, where advancements happen quickly and specialized talents are highly sought for. Personal branding is particularly crucial for developers for the reasons listed below:

- **Difference in a Congested Market:** It can be difficult to distinguish out in the field when thousands of developers enter it every year. With a personal brand, you can showcase not only your abilities but also what makes your method, background, or area of specialization special. A strong brand can highlight your experience and establish you as the go-to person for particular initiatives, regardless of your area of expertise in machine learning, UI/UX design, or cybersecurity.

- **More Employment Possibilities**: Nowadays, a lot of hiring managers and recruiters look beyond the conventional CV. They are looking through personal web pages, GitHub repositories, and LinkedIn profiles to identify applicants who possess both the necessary abilities and the appropriate attitude. Possessing a strong brand increases your marketability and can result in better employment offers, frequently before they are even posted.

- **Establishing Credibility and Trust:** People can tell you're passionate about your career if you have a strong personal brand. Clients, employers, and colleagues are more likely to trust developers with a strong brand. When it comes to landing leadership roles, joint ventures, or freelancing work, trust is essential.

- **Community Engagement and Networking:** Opportunities for deep connections within the developer community arise when you are acknowledged for your competence. Developers who have a strong personal brand are frequently asked to participate in high-profile open-source projects, speak at conferences, or work together on tech blogs. This network may offer career leads, partnerships, or even mentoring.

- **Thought Leadership Opportunities:** A strong brand establishes you as a thought leader in your field, which benefits more than simply your employment prospects. For their views on the newest developments in technology, trends, and industry issues, thought leaders are frequently sought out. These possibilities can greatly advance your career, whether they are through technical interviews, guest articles, or public speaking engagements.

Opportunities for Professional Development and Learning: Building a personal brand necessitates ongoing education and communication. This encourages you to keep abreast of emerging trends, technology, and industry best practices. Participating in the community also yields feedback, which aids in improving your abilities and strategy.

Having a great personal brand in the tech industry increases your recall value, credibility, and desirability in addition to your visibility.

1.3. Typical Myths Regarding Personal Branding

Many developers avoid personal branding because of certain misconceptions, even if it has obvious advantages. Here are some typical ones together with the underlying truth:

"Personal Branding is Just Self-Promotion"

Personal branding, according to many developers, is the same as boasting or continuous self-promotion. But personal branding isn't about bragging; it's about sharing your expertise and effort with others in a genuine and beneficial way. When done right, it's not about boosting your ego but rather about sharing your knowledge and perspectives to benefit your society.

"I Should Only Focus on My Code, Not My Brand"

Although technological know-how is essential, the tech sector looks for more than just basic coding abilities. Soft skills like teamwork, communication, and thought leadership are becoming more and more crucial. You can lose out on chances to showcase your wider strengths and how they help teams or projects succeed if you only concentrate on code.

"Only Senior Developers Need a Personal Brand"

The notion that branding is exclusively for people in high-level or leadership roles is the root of this fallacy. However, a developer can benefit from personal branding at any point in their career. Developing your brand helps you define your professional trajectory and opens doors to new opportunities, regardless of your level of expertise.

"Building a Personal Brand Takes Too Much Time"

Although it takes work to build a personal brand, it doesn't have to be daunting or take up all of your time. Starting small can be as simple as posting a few thoughts on LinkedIn, creating a blog post once a month, or spending your free time working on an open-source project. These little endeavors add up over time to create a strong and identifiable personal brand.

"I Don't Have Anything Unique to Offer"

Many developers believe they lack a distinctive viewpoint or are not special. Actually, each developer has a distinct set of thoughts, challenges, and experiences. You can connect with people who are following similar routes by sharing your journey, whether it's conquering a coding challenge, learning a new language, or integrating new technology.

Developers can gain a better understanding of the actual worth of personal branding and how it can advance their careers by clearing up these myths.

The foundations of personal branding for developers have been covered in this chapter, with an emphasis on how crucial it is to differentiate oneself in a competitive market and debunk common misconceptions that prevent developers from developing their brands. In the rapidly changing world of technology, having a strong, genuine brand is not just a professional advantage but also a tool that can open doors to new opportunities, growth, and collaboration.

CHAPTER 2

ESTABLISHING YOUR OWN DEVELOPER PERSONA

Identifying your own personality is crucial in the technology industry, because each developer contributes an own set of abilities, viewpoints, and experiences. Presenting yourself in a clear, coherent, and captivating manner is made possible by having a clearly defined developer identity. It all comes down to knowing what you have to offer and knowing how to effectively convey that to others, whether they be coworkers, prospective employers, or developers. Finding your fundamental skills, striking a balance between your personal and professional branding, and developing a personal mission statement that captures your special worth are all covered in this chapter.

2.1. Determining Your Fundamental Abilities and Advantages

Knowing what makes you unique is the first step in

establishing your own identity. Finding your fundamental abilities and capabilities is the first step in this process. Knowing which of your many technical skills as a developer best reflect your knowledge and enthusiasm is essential to developing your brand.

How to Determine Your Fundamental Competencies:

1. Evaluate Your Technical Proficiency: Examine the tools, frameworks, and programming languages you know how to use. Do you prefer working as a full-stack, front-end, or back-end developer? Are you an expert in cybersecurity, machine learning, or mobile development?

- Make a list of these technical abilities and rank them according to your comfort level and level of proficiency. Because they will serve as the cornerstone of your brand, think about the technologies you most love using.

2. Assess Your Capabilities for Solving Problems: Consider the kinds of problems you are particularly good at solving outside of coding. Do you have a reputation for enhancing application performance? Or perhaps you are the person that people turn to when they need help

debugging complex systems.
- Don't undervalue this strength; developers that can tackle unusual challenges fast and efficiently tend to stand out.

3. Acknowledge Leadership Qualities and Soft Skills:

Technical proficiency is only one component of the puzzle. Soft skills like leadership, teamwork, and communication are crucial in today's collaborative digital world. Consider this: Can I effectively lead teams or projects?

- Do I have the ability to guide people or communicate difficult ideas to stakeholders who are not technical?
- Can I help cross-functional teams communicate effectively?

4. Get Input from Your Peers:

- Your strengths may not always be as obvious to you as they are to others. Seek input from mentors, clients, or coworkers. Find out what they believe to be your strongest professional and technical attributes. This outside viewpoint can highlight blind spots or validate areas that require attention.

5. Examine Your Areas of Passion: Lastly, consider what most thrills you. Your passions and areas of competence are not the only things that constitute your fundamental strengths. You will have the greatest influence and take pleasure in your career when your passions and talents meet.

You may better understand the abilities that make you a developer and form the cornerstone of your distinct identity by determining your primary competencies.

2.2. Branding: Personal vs. Professional Identity

Finding a balance between their personal and professional identities is one of the difficulties developers have when developing their personal brands. Although both are significant facets of your identity, how you combine them can either strengthen or weaken your brand. Let's examine how to successfully strike this equilibrium.

Recognizing Professional and Personal Identity: Professional Identity:

In a formal professional environment, you should look like this. It encompasses your abilities, background, work ethic, and technical project contributions. Your job title and position within your organization, the technology you use at work, and the professional values you uphold like accountability, integrity, and teamwork all serve to create your professional identity.

Identity of the Individual:

This includes the distinctive qualities, passions, and principles that define your identity outside of the workplace. It encompasses your interests, philosophy of life, communication style, and approach to difficulties or learning. Your personal identification can affect the following:

- The tone of your online presence (e.g., blogs, social media)
- How you engage with peers in the IT community
- Your more general technological interests, such as areas of experimentation or curiosity unrelated to your current position

Integrating Your Personal and Professional Brands:

Preserve Authenticity:

Your true self as a person and as a developer should be reflected in your personal brand. Since authenticity promotes engagement and trust, it is essential. Maintaining professionalism is crucial, but don't be scared to show off a little of your personality, especially if it fits with your brand's core principles. For example, incorporate your enthusiasm for mentoring young engineers or participating in open-source initiatives into your brand narrative.

Adapt Information to the Viewers:

Understanding your audience is just as crucial as being real. Stress your technical proficiency, problem-solving skills, and teamwork or project contributions in professional contexts. Feel free to offer personal thoughts or lessons acquired when interacting with larger audiences (on tech blogs or social media), provided that they are pertinent and valuable.

Utilize Personal Narratives to Advance Your Career:

Humanizing your brand can be achieved by sharing your personal story, such as how you learnt a challenging technology, solved a project obstacle, or why you decided to become a developer. These anecdotes provide your professional accomplishments perspective and increase the relatability of your brand.

Keep in Mind Your Boundaries:
Finding a balance between being transparent and upholding professionalism is crucial. Share personal stories that fit your professional persona, but steer clear of anything that can come out as excessively informal or unrelated to your brand.

In the end, a stronger and more relatable brand might result from carefully combining your personal and professional identities. Finding a peaceful solution to allow them to coexist is more important than picking one over the other.

2.3 Making a Personal Mission Statement

A strong tool for establishing your developer identity and directing your professional decisions is a personal goal statement. It acts as a North Star, assisting you in keeping your priorities in mind and coordinating your activities with your long-term objectives. Your values, interests, and purpose are succinctly and clearly expressed in a well-written mission statement.

The Significance of a Personal Mission Statement:

Elucidates Your Objective:

You can better understand your motivations by creating a mission statement. It compels you to reflect carefully on your objectives, the difference you hope to make, and the ways in which you will support the IT community.

Informs Career Choices:

Your goal statement can assist direct your selections while you're assessing learning possibilities, choosing a side project, or accepting a job offer. It guarantees that the decisions you make are consistent with your values, both personal and professional.

The way you convey your vision to others:

It's easier for people to comprehend your values and passions when you have a specific mission statement. Your mission statement serves as a concise means of introducing your values and goals to everyone, be it a follower, coworker, or prospective employer.

How to Write a Powerful Statement of Personal Mission:

1. Examine Your Passions and Values:
Consider your motivations as a developer first. What principles drive your work? What about coding most interests you? Do you want to create technologies that address practical issues? Or do you have a strong desire to guide the upcoming generation of developers?

2. Establish Your Career Objectives:
Think about your desired future self. What are your long-term professional objectives? Do you want to work as a team leader, create cutting-edge products, or support open-source communities? Your mission statement needs to represent both your current goals and your long-term objectives.

3. Determine the influence You Wish to Make:
Effective mission statements emphasize the wider influence you hope to achieve rather than just your daily

activities. Consider the following:
- How can I help the IT community?
- What kind of legacy am I hoping to leave?
- How will the lives of others be enhanced by my work?

The fourth step is to make it concise and actionable: Your goal statement should be brief enough to be easily remembered, yet comprehensive enough to offer guidance. Choose one or two sentences that succinctly convey your goal. Make use of powerful action verbs that convey your determination and dedication.

Sample Developer Personal Mission Statements:
- "To develop scalable, user-friendly software that improves user experiences and enables people to accomplish their objectives."
- "To continuously learn and apply cutting-edge technologies to solve complex problems, while mentoring others to grow in their technical journeys."
- "To lead creative projects that foster growth and positive change in the tech community by bridging

the gap between technology and human needs."

A personal mission statement is a statement of your purpose as a developer, not just a catchphrase. It acts as a compass, guiding you purposefully and confidently along your professional path.

This chapter has covered how to create a personal goal statement, balance professional and personal branding, and discover your core talents in order to construct your distinct developer identity. By presenting oneself as an influential, focused, and genuine developer, each phase helps you build a strong personal brand that appeals to the IT sector.

CHAPTER 3

CREATING A RECURRING MESSAGE AND THEME

It takes more than just technical expertise to stand out as a developer in today's cluttered digital market; you also need a unified personal brand that tells an engaging story. Developing a consistent theme and message involves balancing your visual presentation, your communication tone and voice, and making sure that your online and offline presence reflect your identity and key values. This chapter explores how to develop consistency across all platforms and the components that make up a powerful, cohesive personal brand.

3.1 Selecting a Uniform Visual Identity

The first thing prospective employers, partners, and your audience see about you is your visual identity. Your visual identity as a developer includes everything from the colors, typefaces, and images you select to the layout of your portfolio, social media accounts, and website. Maintaining consistency in these visual components strengthens your brand and increases your recall and recognition.

The Significance of Visual Identity:

First Impressions:
Your visual identity establishes the tone for how people view you, whether they are viewing your website, LinkedIn page, or social media feed. Credibility and attention to detail are communicated through a polished and expert visual identity.

It is easier for people to remember you when you employ visual components like a logo, color scheme, and typography consistently. Consider it as creating your signature style, similar to how businesses have identifiable logos and brand colors.

The value of professionalism:
A strong visual identity demonstrates your commitment to your brand. It shows not just how you like to look but also how professional you are and how you approach your

business.

Essential Components of a Powerful Visual Identity:

1. Branding and Logo:
- Even while you might not require a complicated logo as a developer, having a clear and uncomplicated visual representation of your business can help set you apart. This might be a symbol that reflects your proficiency with code, or it could be your initials in a distinctive typeface.
- If creating a logo sounds overwhelming, think about hiring a graphic designer or using online tools to make a logo that is appropriate for your company.

2. Color Palette:
- Pick a color palette that goes well with your style or the mood of your work. For instance:
- Vibrant hues can convey vitality and inventiveness.
- Neutral, subdued tones exude dependability and expertise.
- Darker hues might stand for technical proficiency or sophistication.

- To establish a unified look, stick to a palette of two to three primary colors and utilize them consistently on your website, portfolio, and social media accounts.

3. Typography:
- Your visual identity is greatly influenced by your typography. Select typefaces that complement the personality of your brand and are clear and readable.
- To ensure uniformity across platforms, limit your font usage to one or two (for example, one for headings and another for body text).

4. Imagery and Visual Content:
Your brand should be reflected in the photos you use on your website, blog, and social media accounts. For example:
- Make use of high-quality headshots for your profile photos.
- Make sure the project photos you use are crisp and of the highest caliber to present your work in the best possible light.
- If you choose to utilize illustrations, make sure they

complement the professional or informal tone of your brand.

Establishing Consistency Across Platforms: Make sure that the visual identity components used on your website, portfolio, and social media profiles are the same to provide a smooth experience for users interacting with your business through various channels.

- Smaller details, such as business cards or email signatures, should be incorporated into your overall visual identity.

Maintaining consistency and intentionality in your visual presentation is crucial since, at its core, your visual identity is a reflection of your technical prowess, expertise, and inventiveness.

3.2. Establishing a Harmonious Voice and Tone

Just as crucial as your visual identity is the voice and tone you employ in your communications. When combined, they aid in building a unified and identifiable brand that captures your character, principles, and expertise. Having a distinct tone and voice guarantees that your message is consistently in line with your personal brand, whether you're writing blog entries, engaging on social media, or making presentations at conferences.

Establishing Your Voice and Tone:

Voice:

The consistent personality or style that permeates your communications is known as your voice. On several systems, it stays comparatively steady. For example:

- Do you write in a formal or informal manner?
- Do you emphasize instruction and informational content, or do you also include humor and anecdotes?

Tone:

Conversely, your tone can vary based on the audience or situation. For instance, you may speak more casually on social media yet use a more formal tone in a job interview or technical blog post.

How to Develop a Harmonious Voice and Tone:

1. get to know your audience: Consider your target audience before deciding on your voice and tone. Are other developers your intended audience? Customers who aren't techies? Possible employers? Adapt your communication style to their requirements and expectations.

2. Complement Your Personality: Your speech and tone should reflect your true self. As long as it fits with your career objectives, it's acceptable to let your brand reflect your inherent humor and laid-backness. On the other hand, utilize a tone that conveys your technical depth and precision if you are more reserved and analytical.

3. Maintain Uniformity Across Platforms: Your voice and tone should be constant whether you're posting on LinkedIn, tweeting about your most recent project, or writing code documentation. This means keeping a consistent style and attitude rather than utilizing the same words in every post.

4. Maintain a Balance Between Professionalism and Approachability: You must mix professionalism and approachability in your work as a developer. For example:

- You may demonstrate your expertise while making difficult technical ideas easy for people to understand by explaining them in your blog entries.
- You can take a more laid-back approach on social media, offering insights or interacting with your audience in a warm and approachable manner.

The fifth step is to create core messaging concepts that are consistent with your own brand. These are broad principles or ideals that direct your speech and delivery. For instance:

- Sharing the newest technologies you're investigating is an example of innovation.
- Collaborating: Emphasizing projects in which you have collaborated with others.

Problem-Solving: Exhibiting how you tackle difficulties and come up with answers.

- These themes will assist you in maintaining concentration and guarantee that your communications consistently advance your more general objectives.

You can maintain the professionalism needed in the IT sector while creating a more approachable and human brand by creating a consistent tone and voice. Whether you're addressing a thousand people or just one, it all comes down to striking your own balance and making sure your message is consistent.

3.3 Aligning Your Online and Offline Presence

A well-rounded developer identity is present in both your online and real encounters. Building authenticity and trust requires that your online persona be consistent with your in-person professional image. Reinforcing your personal brand requires consistency in all interactions, whether you're working with coworkers, networking at meetups, or attending conferences.

The Importance of Online and Offline Presence Alignment

Establishes Authenticity and Trust:
Maintaining a consistent online and offline presence helps you gain the audience's trust. Your credibility may suffer if your online persona portrays you as personable, creative, and meticulous, but in person you come across as

haphazard or aloof.

The following strengthens brand recognition:

People should feel as though they are meeting the same person they have seen online when they meet you in person. This increases your recall value and strengthens your brand.

Builds Professional Connections:

Additionally, consistency fosters stronger bonds between people. People you meet offline, whether at conferences, interviews, or during partnerships, will feel more connected to you if your online persona is genuine.

Getting Your Offline and Online Presence in Line:

1. Be genuine on the internet: Being authentic begins with your online persona. It might be challenging to live up to your online image in real-life interactions if it is an overly dramatic or meticulously manicured representation of who you are. Rather, concentrate on creating an online persona that accurately represents your identity, values, and working style.

2. Rehearse Your Real-World Communication Style:

Use these techniques in your offline contacts if your online brand places a strong emphasis on succinct and clear communication. Speaking at conferences, meeting possible employers, or participating in networking activities can all benefit from this. Make sure your voice and tone translate into in-person conversations.

3. Maintain Consistent Professional principles:

Your offline work should reflect the principles you express online, such as creativity, teamwork, and ongoing learning. For example:

- Show that you value online collaboration by participating in team initiatives and interacting with coworkers during meetings.
- Make sure you keep taking advantage of professional development opportunities, including attending workshops or mentoring others, if you advocate for the value of learning and development.

4. Make Use of Offline possibilities to Expand Your Online Presence:

Enhance your online brand by utilizing offline possibilities.

For instance:

- If you go to conferences, write a blog article or post on social media with your thoughts or key takeaways.
- Share images or updates from events to demonstrate your involvement with the larger tech community. By bridging the gap between your online and offline lives, these initiatives help your brand feel more cohesive and complete.

5. Make connections and cultivate relationships: In addition to how you portray yourself, how other people view and discuss you also contributes to the reinforcement of your personal brand. Engage in physical and online networking, and be receptive to establishing new business connections. People are more inclined to interact with your online material and recommend you to others when they know and trust you in real-world situations.

Coordinating your online and real presence guarantees that you project an image of professionalism, authenticity, and dependability across your personal brand. It's about making sure that everyone who engages with you, whether in person or on a screen, has a smooth experience. When done correctly, this alignment improves credibility, fortifies your reputation, and creates new prospects in the tech industry.

CHAPTER 4

PUTTING TOGETHER A STRONG PORTFOLIO

Your portfolio serves as the online representation of your development brand and is more than just a list of your completed projects. One of the most important components of your personal brand is your portfolio, which can make the difference between getting hired and being passed over. This chapter will cover how to create a portfolio that not only highlights your technical proficiency but also narrates your capacity for creativity, problem-solving, and career potential. We'll go over the essential components of any developer portfolio, effective presentation techniques, and the top resources and platforms for building a distinctive portfolio.

4.1 Important Components of a Developer Portfolio

A strong portfolio accomplishes two goals: it showcases your technical prowess and illustrates how you tackle real-world issues. Not only do prospective employers, clients, or partners want to see that you can create code, but they also want to know how you think, collaborate with others, and turn your abilities into useful results.

Crucial Elements:

1. Bio/Introduction:
- The first section of your portfolio should be a succinct bio that tells visitors about yourself, your experience, and your motivations as a developer. This section should be brief but intimate, including details on your development journey, your enthusiasm for technology, and your primary competencies.
- Emphasize significant accomplishments or turning points in your career that provide context for your career path.

2. Overview of Skills:
- Give a concise synopsis of the technical abilities, resources, and frameworks you use. Employers can see what languages, libraries, and technologies you

are skilled in by looking at this area, which provides a quick overview of your primary competencies.

Consider carefully organizing this area by classifying the skills into groups like:

- **Front-End Development:** HTML, CSS, JavaScript, React
- **Back-End Development:** Node.js, Python, Django, databases
- **DevOps:** Docker, Kubernetes, CI/CD
- **Cloud Services:** GCP, AWS, and Azure

3. Case Studies/Projects:

- Your projects are the focal point of your portfolio. This is your chance to highlight your accomplishments, methods, and methods for completing each job. Listing projects is insufficient; you also need to provide an explanation of each one's backstory.

Include the following for every project:

- **Problem Statement:** What issue were you trying to solve?

- **Your Role:** What particular contribution did you make? Did you oversee the project or were you a team member?
- **Result:** What was the outcome? If at all possible, include metrics (e.g., increased traffic by Y users, improved performance by X%).
- **Difficulties and Resolutions:** Describe any obstacles you faced and how you resolved them. This illustrates your capacity for critical analysis and problem-solving.

Testimonials/References:
- If at all possible, include endorsements from previous customers, employers, or coworkers. Positive comments serve as social proof to prospective customers or recruiting managers, reaffirming the caliber of your work.
- If you have made contributions to open-source projects, think about mentioning concerns or contributions where other developers have commended you.

5. Call to Action/Contact Details:

- Make it simple for guests to contact you. Offer a variety of ways to get in touch, including email, LinkedIn, and a contact form. This is particularly crucial if you're trying to find networking or freelancing possibilities.
- To encourage participation, provide a clear call to action, such as "Let's work together" or "Contact me for collaborations."

6. Optional Thought Leadership or Blog Section:

- A blog or section where you share ideas, tutorials, or insights into industry trends can significantly improve your portfolio, however it is not required. It establishes you as a thinking leader and demonstrates your continued interest in the newest technological advancements. Frequent blog entries on development-related subjects can help highlight your aptitude for succinctly communicating complicated concepts, which is a useful asset in many tech positions.

By making sure your portfolio includes these essential components, you provide prospective employers and partners with a thorough understanding of your abilities, background, and development methodology.

4.2. Highlighting Your Contributions and Projects

The projects you highlight are the foundation of any developer portfolio. These are not merely samples of your work; they also show how you use your technical expertise to address practical issues. This section will explore ways to showcase your contributions and projects in a way that best showcases your abilities and capabilities.

Choosing Appropriate Projects:

Quality Over Quantity:
The finest portfolios prioritize quality over quantity, despite the temptation to include every project you've ever worked on. Select tasks that best reflect your present skill set and the kind of work you hope to be recruited for.

Diverse Skill Sets: Choose projects that demonstrate a variety of abilities. For instance, to show off your versatility, include both front-end and back-end projects if you specialize in full-stack development.

Impact on the Real World:

Emphasize initiatives that made a quantifiable difference for a client, the open-source community, or your own development. If at all possible, provide metrics or user comments that demonstrate the project's success, such as "built a feature that increased user engagement by 30%" or "improved page load times by 50%."

Putting Project Descriptions in Order:

1. Title and Brief Overview:

- Begin with a concise one-line synopsis that captures the project's goal and a clear project title.

2. Issue and Resolution:

- Every project needs a story. Give a detailed explanation of the issue you were trying to solve and the solution you came up with. This enables people to comprehend the situation and observe how you solve problems.

3. Contributions and Role:

- Describe your work on each project in detail. For instance: "Used React to design and implement the front-end, improving UI/UX."
- "Oversaw database architecture and API integrations while leading back-end development."
- Emphasize your unique contributions, particularly while working on group projects.

4. Difficulties and Learnings:
- Talk about any difficulties you had and how you overcame them. This can be a time limitation, a technical problem, or a new technology you have to pick up quickly. You can differentiate yourself from other developers by demonstrating how you overcome challenges.

5. Code Samples and Visuals:
- Whenever feasible, provide live demos, videos, or screenshots of your work. Visual tools provide guests a concrete understanding of your job. To allow interested individuals to learn more about your technical contributions, pair this with links to your GitHub repository or pertinent code snippets.

Highlighting Community and Open-Source Contributions:

Open-Source Contributions:
Make sure to include open-source projects in your portfolio if you contribute to them. Add issue tracking, pull requests, and any noteworthy exchanges with other developers.

Community Involvement:
Emphasize any contributions you have made to development communities, such as mentoring young developers, creating tutorials, or taking part in hackathons. This shows dedication to the development ecosystem, leadership, and teamwork.

In conclusion, exhibiting your efforts is more than just showing off the finished item; it's also about sharing the journey you took, the difficulties you encountered, and the solutions you came up with. This method enables prospective employers to observe not only your technical proficiency but also your ability to think creatively, solve problems, and solve problems.

4.3. Resources and Systems for Developing Your Portfolio

Selecting the appropriate platform to display your work is just as important as creating compelling content for your portfolio. The design, functionality, and user experience of your portfolio can be greatly influenced by the platforms and tools you use to create it. The top platforms and tools for developers will be discussed in this area, along with factors to take into account when selecting the ideal platform for your requirements.

Well-known platforms for portfolios:

1. GitHub Pages:
Reasons to Use It:
- Developers can host static web pages straight from their GitHub projects using the free platform GitHub Pages. Developers are drawn to it since it's perfect for displaying both your technical documents and coding tasks.
- **Best For:** developers that prefer a simple, code-first

method of portfolio development. It's especially helpful if you wish to host your project documentation or showcase open-source contributions.

The second is Netlify:

Why Use It:

For static websites, Netlify provides scalable and quick hosting. Because of its good integration with GitHub, web apps and portfolios may be deployed with ease. Netlify is a versatile option for more complex portfolios because of its integrated features, which include form processing and authentication.

- **Best For:** Developers that want greater control over the functionality and performance of their portfolio, such as those creating intricate or dynamic front-end projects.

3. Why Use It:

WordPress:

One of the most widely used content management systems (CMS) is WordPress, which offers extensive customization options. Its many themes, plugins, and widgets make it simple to create a portfolio that is both aesthetically pleasing and useful without requiring much knowledge of front-end development.

- **Best For:** Developers that like a portfolio that is easily adaptable and emphasizes design flexibility and ease of use above coding.

4. Webflow:

The Reasons for Using It:

Using a visual interface, Webflow's no-code platform lets developers create unique websites while giving them direct access to the code for further customization. Technical control and design freedom are well-balanced.

- **Best For:** developers that require the ability to work with the code but also desire a portfolio that is visually appealing and design-focused.

5. Squarespace:

- **Reasons to Use It:** Squarespace provides a simplified, low-tech method for building expert websites. It is a popular option for developers who like to concentrate more on content and less on technical setup because of its eye-catching

templates.
- Developers who want a plug-and-play solution with expert design aesthetics are the ideal candidates.

Personalized Portfolio Websites:
Creating From the Ground Up:

Creating a custom portfolio from the ground up might be a fantastic choice for developers who desire total control over the layout, features, and user experience of their portfolio. You can make a totally original web presence with tools like HTML, CSS, JavaScript, and frameworks like React or Vue.js.

The Reason to Customize:

Although WordPress and GitHub Pages are convenient, creating a unique portfolio highlights your design and programming abilities in addition to your projects. A custom-built portfolio can be a great distinction when applying for jobs in front-end development, UX/UI design, or any other field where aesthetics are important.

Important Things to Look for When Selecting a Platform:

Customization vs. Usability:

Although they are simple to set up, platforms like Squarespace and WordPress provide less control than creating your portfolio from the ground up. Custom websites, on the other hand, offer the most control but demand more technical know-how and time.

Performance & Scalability:

Platforms like Netlify or GitHub Pages, which provide developers with superior performance and scalability, are worth considering if you want your portfolio to manage high traffic or house intricate projects (like interactive demos).

It is important to make sure that the platform you select supports mobile-responsive design. Your portfolio will be viewed by many people on mobile devices, therefore it's important that your work works and looks fantastic on all screen sizes.

Maintenance: Think about how much time you wish to devote to portfolio maintenance. The majority of backend maintenance is handled by platforms like Webflow or

Squarespace, but custom-built portfolios need more constant work to stay current.

Creating a strong developer portfolio involves a combination of demonstrating your technical proficiency, organizing your work in an engaging manner, and selecting the appropriate platform to showcase your creations. Regardless of whether you choose a pre-made platform or start from scratch, your portfolio should showcase not only your abilities but also your drive for growth, your aptitude for overcoming problems, and your willingness to take on new challenges.

CHAPTER 5

Producing Content That Shows Off Your Knowledge

One of the best methods to position oneself as an authority in your industry in the current digital environment is to provide content. Being able to share your expertise through different types of content can boost your professional visibility and draw in chances, regardless of whether you are a developer, data scientist, or tech enthusiast. With an emphasis on blogging, video lessons, and participating in industry forums, this chapter will examine how to produce material that shows your knowledge and is meaningful. We'll go into tactics for producing powerful content that establishes you as a thought leader while simultaneously educating your audience.

5.1. Blogging: Exchanging Experiences and Knowledge

One of the easiest and most efficient ways for professionals to communicate their expertise is through blogging. A well-written blog post has the power to connect with readers, address particular issues, and offer insightful information about your field. Regular blogging can help you build your professional identity and give you a stage on which to demonstrate your knowledge, ideas, and problem-solving abilities.

The Significance of Blogging:

Establishes Authority:

You become an authority by writing frequently about your field, tools, or particular technology. Readers start to link your name to trustworthy, perceptive content, which may result in offers of employment, speaking engagements, or freelancing chances.

Enhances Communication Abilities:

Writing compels you to simplify difficult concepts, which improves your communication skills. Clear explanation of technical ideas is a useful competence, particularly in positions requiring teaching or teamwork.

Improves Exposure:

Content is highly valued by search engines. Your blog entries will show up in search engine results if they are properly optimized with pertinent keywords and useful content. This raises your internet presence over time, increasing website traffic and enhancing your reputation in the workplace.

How to Begin Writing a Blog:

1. Select a Niche:

Despite the temptation to write about everything you're interested in, concentrate on the area in which you are most knowledgeable. Having a narrow specialization, whether it is AI, data analytics, or a certain programming language, speeds up the process of establishing your authority.

Some examples of niches include:

- Front-end development with Vue.js or React

- Python data visualization approaches
- Best practices for cybersecurity in startups

2. Identify Your Target Audience:

Knowing who your target audience is is essential. Do you write for seasoned pros, novices, or intermediate students? Address the questions they are likely to ask in order to customize your material to meet their needs.

3. Produce Useful, Actionable Content:

The reader should truly benefit from your blog. Go into detail rather than just general guidance. Problem-solving blogs, case studies, tutorials, and how-tos are the most effective because they provide readers with useful insights they can implement.

Actionable blog post examples include:

- "How to Create a Basic REST API in Node.js"
- "React Application Memory Leak Debugging"
- "A Comprehensive Overview of Feature

Engineering in Machine Learning"

4. Maintain Consistency:

Building an audience requires consistency. Whether it's one post per week or two posts per month, set a realistic content schedule and follow it. By being consistent, you gain the audience's trust and become recognized as an authority on the subject.

5. Search Engine Optimization (SEO) Optimization:

Make sure your blog entries can be found by concentrating on SEO techniques such as:

- Incorporating pertinent keywords organically into the text
- Creating click-baiting meta descriptions for users
- Using headings (H1, H2, and H3) to organize your post for improved reading and search engine optimization
- Increasing the authority of the material by utilizing both internal and external links

Keeping Your Blog Interesting:

Engage with the readers:

Interact with readers who value your work by leaving comments and answering their inquiries. This demonstrates that you are not only informed but also personable.

Continually Update Content:

Some blog entries may become out of date as technology advances. To keep earlier posts accurate and relevant, make it a habit to go back and update them with new information.

Blogging by Guests:

Consider guest posting on more well-known industry websites after you have started your own blog. This makes you more visible and gives you access to a larger audience.

Blogging is a flexible and effective way to interact with the community, offer your expertise, and establish your authority. Your blog can become an essential part of your personal brand if you are consistent, provide great information, and engage your audience.

5.2. Making Use of Video Tutorials and YouTube

Video has become one of the most popular and interesting ways to study and consume information, even though written content is still crucial. YouTube videos are a great method for developers and technical professionals to demonstrate their skills, simplify difficult subjects, and reach a wider audience. Video tutorials offer a more engaging method of imparting knowledge, whether you're describing complex data models, guiding through code, or setting up a development environment.

Video Content's Power:

Visual Education:

A lot of people learn best visually. Technical procedures can be shown on video, which can be far more impactful than a written explanation. Visualizations, live problem-solving, and code walkthroughs facilitate viewer comprehension.

Increased Involvement:

Higher engagement rates are frequently the result of videos. A well-made video instructional has a higher chance of being shared and commented on by users than a blog post, which expands your audience and visibility.

The Human Connection:

A video gives you a personality. A more intimate bond is formed when viewers witness and hear you discuss subjects. Building trust can be facilitated by this, particularly if you regularly produce lucid, perceptive content.

How to Make YouTube Tutorials That Work:

1. Make a Content Plan:

Choose a topic first that fits the needs of your audience and your area of expertise. Concentrate on resolving a particular issue or elucidating a certain idea. Your video will have a clear framework if you plan your topic in advance.

2. Write an outline or script:

Even though some people like to wing it, having a script or thorough plan helps you stay organized and focused. It makes sure you don't ramble or omit important ideas, which makes your writing more polished and readable.

3. Install High-Grade Recording Equipment:

Video quality is important. Although you don't need a lot of pricey equipment to get started, make sure your video has clear audio and adequate lighting. A good camera and microphone combination can greatly improve the viewing experience.

For tutorials that are screen recorded, record your desktop using programs like OBS Studio or Camtasia, making sure that any code or slides are visible.

4. Give a clear and concise explanation:

Steer clear of jargon and simplify your explanations excessively. Make the assumption that your audience may not be as knowledgeable as you are, and go over ideas step-by-step. Make complex concepts easy to understand by using analogies or real-world experiences.

5. Explain Practical Uses:

When viewers witness a concept or technology in action, their level of engagement increases. When showcasing a JavaScript library, for instance, demonstrate how to use it to create a useful feature in a web application.

6. Polish and edit:

To produce a video that looks professional, editing is essential. Eliminate any errors, unneeded pauses, and digressions. To improve comprehension, use captions, diagrams, or annotations.

7. Tube optimization:

Your video tutorials should be search engine optimized, just like your blog entries. Make sure your content is discoverable by using clear video descriptions, pertinent tags, and descriptive titles. Click-through rates can also be greatly impacted by captivating titles and thumbnails.

Advantages of Having a YouTube Account:

Possibilities for Monetization:

YouTube provides a number of options for making money off of your material after you've developed a following, such as affiliate marketing, sponsored videos, and ad revenue.

Developing a Base of Subscribers:

More constant viewership and engagement might result

from having a foundation of devoted subscribers. Frequently, subscribers turn into recurring viewers, which gradually increases your influence.

Collaboration & Networking:

You can be asked to work with other YouTubers, developers, or businesses as your channel expands. New chances like collaborations, speaking engagements, or special projects become possible as a result.

Using YouTube to produce video tutorials is a great method to reach a larger audience, interact with them, and present your abilities in a more engaging way. Video content may greatly improve your professional brand, whether you're making straightforward tutorials or comprehensive video courses.

5.3. Participating in Forums and Industry Discussions

Another great method to demonstrate your expertise is to participate in industry debates on forums, social media, and community platforms in addition to producing your own material. You may exchange ideas, find solutions to issues, and position yourself as an authority in your field by interacting with people in your profession. These contributions show your dedication to the larger IT community, whether you're answering inquiries, taking part in technical conversations, or working on open-source projects.

Reasons to Participate in Industry Conversations:

Networking Possibilities:

Talking with others creates opportunities to network with influencers, other professionals, and possible partners. Engaging actively in forums and conversations facilitates the development of relationships with people who share your interests and viewpoints.

Ongoing Education:

Participating in conversations allows you to learn from others as well as share your knowledge. Since the tech sector is always changing, networking with colleagues helps you stay up to date on the latest technologies, trends, and best practices.

Improving Reputation:

Regularly offering considerate, perceptive responses to technical inquiries or participating in intricate conversations will increase your standing within the sector. People will begin to see you as an informed and trustworthy source.

Location of Engagement:

1. stack overflow

Stack Overflow, one of the most well-known developer platforms, lets you respond to technical and coding queries. You may show off your knowledge and raise your profile in the developer community by offering solutions to actual issues.

2. Subreddits for Technology and Development:

Developers, data scientists, and tech aficionados can exchange ideas, pose questions, and talk about industry trends in the many technology-related subreddits on Reddit. You can increase your following by posting insightful comments or responding to queries in subreddits such as r/programming or r/machinelearning.

3. Twitter:

Twitter is an effective way to interact with the larger IT community. You may create a professional network and position yourself as a thought leader by taking part in topical debates (like #DevDiscuss) and providing industry news and views.

4. Discussions on GitHub:

Developers may now work together on projects, ask questions, and provide feedback using GitHub's discussion function. One excellent method to support the open-source community is to participate in GitHub conversations, particularly in repositories that are pertinent to your area of expertise.

5. Quora:

Another site where you can respond to inquiries about your field of expertise is Quora. Because of the platform's extensive coverage of various subjects, you can also demonstrate your expertise to a non-technical audience.

Techniques for Contributions That Have Meaning:

Maintain Consistency:

Similar to writing a blog or making videos, consistency is essential. To increase long-term visibility, regularly take part in conversations, give guidance, and interact with people in your field.

Offer Value:

Make an effort to provide insightful, useful guidance. Provide thorough explanations, snippets of code, or resources that can assist in resolving particular issues rather than general responses.

Remain Professional:

Even in informal settings, keep your tone professional. Since your contributions represent your personal brand, it's critical to project an air of deference, expertise, and friendliness.

Encourage thoughtful conversations:

Encourage conversations by posing follow-up queries or offering different viewpoints rather than merely responding to inquiries. This promotes more in-depth community involvement.

Participating in industry forums and debates is a great approach to establish your credibility, connect with other professionals, and keep up with developments in the field. By continuously making significant contributions, you establish yourself as a major force in your industry and learn from your colleagues.

Building a solid professional presence requires producing material that showcases your knowledge, whether it be through industry talks, video lessons, or blogging. In addition to showcasing your abilities, you can make a significant contribution to the advancement of your business by exchanging knowledge, interacting with the community, and regularly creating worthwhile content.

CHAPTER 6

Building a Powerful Social Media Presence

For professionals who wish to stand out in today's digitally first world, having a strong social media presence is now essential. More than just a means of communication, social media platforms give a priceless chance to network with colleagues in the field, exhibit expertise, and build one's personal brand. A carefully managed social media presence can lead to thought leadership, job prospects, and collaborations.

This chapter will walk you through the process of choosing the appropriate channels, using techniques to develop a loyal following, and maintaining your professional image on important social media sites like GitHub, LinkedIn, and Twitter.

6.1. Selecting Appropriate Social Media Channels

Establishing a focused, expert online presence requires selecting the appropriate social media channels. Not all platforms are made equal, so concentrating on the networks that fit your audience, goals, and industry will improve the results of your efforts. Knowing the advantages of each platform can help you make wise choices because they all support various kinds of content, engagement preferences, and career options.

Comprehending Platform Dynamics

Take into account the following features of each social media site before choosing the best one:

1. LinkedIn:
- **Goal:** Industry news, thought leadership, and professional networking.
- **Audience:** Industry leaders, executives, recruiters, and business professionals.
- **Content Type:** Job advertisements, industry insights, professional updates, personal accomplishments, and articles.

Professional groups, company pages, LinkedIn learning,

and articles are some of the main features.

The platform of choice for professionals in any area is LinkedIn. It functions as an industry-specific knowledge dissemination hub, networking tool, and online resume. Professionals can establish credibility on LinkedIn by posting thoughtful articles, updates on significant career events, and thought leadership on market trends.

2. Twitter (or X):
- **Goal:** Instantaneous interaction, industry conversations, and prompt updates.
- The audience consists of journalists, influencers, tech enthusiasts, business owners, and members of the general public.
- Short-form postings, news updates, threads (in-depth debates), and live commentary are examples of the content type. Hashtags, trending topics, Twitter Spaces (live audio conversations), and lists are some of the main features.

Twitter is ideal for sharing news, ideas, and participating in real-time conversations since it relies on brief, succinct communication. In tech circles, the site is widely utilized, especially for following prominent figures in the field, keeping up with current events, and taking part in debates about cutting-edge subjects like artificial intelligence, blockchain, and programming frameworks.

3. GitHub:

- **Goal:** Sharing coding projects and fostering collaborative software development.
- Data scientists, software engineers, developers, and IT recruiters make up the audience.
- **Content Type:** Open-source contributions, coding challenges, project documentation, and repositories.
- GitHub Discussions, Pull Requests, Issues, and Project Pages are among its primary features.

GitHub is a platform that combines software development with social interaction. Although hosting and organizing code is its main function, developers can also make an impression by exhibiting their own work, taking part in conversations, and contributing to open-source projects.

The purpose of Instagram is to provide visual images,

share behind-the-scenes stories, and promote personal branding.

- **Audience:** The general public, designers, entrepreneurs, and creatives.
- **Content Type**:NPictures, IGTV (long-form video), Stories, and short videos (Reels).
- Reels, IGTV, Stories, and Highlights are some of the main features.

Instagram has grown in popularity as a medium for designers, UI/UX experts, and other creative professionals to display their portfolios and personal projects, despite its conventional associations with lifestyle and visual storytelling.

5. YouTube:

- **Audience:** Professionals, learners, creators, and the general public
- Purpose: Video content and lessons.
- **Content Type:** Product reviews, webinars, vlogs, tutorials, and instructional materials.

Playlists, Live Streams, Community Tabs, and YouTube Shorts are some of the main features.

For professionals that can provide instructional or educational video, YouTube is the perfect place. YouTube is frequently used by developers to share live coding sessions, code walkthroughs, and lessons.

Matching Platforms to Your Objectives

Align your social media activities with your career objectives after you have a clear understanding of each platform's target audience and purpose. Consider this:

- Do I wish to impart my expertise and perspectives to other professionals? Twitter and LinkedIn might be the finest.
- Do I want to work with others on technical projects or present them? Pay attention to GitHub and perhaps Twitter.
- Do I want to use creativity and design as the foundation of my personal brand? YouTube and Instagram are great for that.

Building meaningful involvement where it counts most can be achieved by concentrating on two to three platforms instead of overstretching yourself across them all.

6.2. Methods for Developing an Active Audience

Although it takes time and work to develop an active social media following, the benefits can be substantial. In addition to spreading your message, a committed, engaged audience may be a resource for networking and teamwork. The following tactics will boost engagement, foster trust, and help you develop your following naturally.

The Key Is Consistency

Consistency is one of the most important factors in developing a social media following. By regularly publishing high-quality material, you can keep your audience's attention. Decide on a timetable that suits you, whether it be monthly video uploads, weekly articles, or daily posts. Being consistent conveys professionalism and dedication.

To ensure a consistent flow of material, plan your posts ahead of time by creating a content calendar. Themes, events, and important dates for post creation can be arranged with the aid of a content calendar.

For instance:

- Monday: Provide an update on a new project or blog post.
- Wednesday: Take part in a Twitter conversation or hot subject.
- Friday: Share a motivational saying or work-related insight.

Give Your Audience Something of Value

The goal of your social media presence should always be to benefit your audience. Share information, tools, advice, and insights that help your followers advance their knowledge or abilities rather than just promoting yourself. By concentrating on offering solutions to typical industry problems, you'll draw in a more interested audience.

The following are practical advice and how-tos: Make material that tackles actual issues facing your sector. Sharing how-to tips, walkthroughs, and tutorials is a great way to interact with your followers and demonstrate your knowledge.

- For instance, a developer may share a thread on Twitter that includes code snippets and instructions for resolving a typical coding issue.

In addition to demonstrating your problem-solving skills, sharing real-world case studies from your professional or personal initiatives enables followers to get insight from your experiences.

Get Active in Your Neighborhood

Social media is about establishing connections, not simply sharing stuff. Whether it's by answering comments, taking part in conversations, or working with others, interacting with your audience fosters a more devoted and involved following.

Answer Questions and Comments:
- Try your best to answer followers' queries or comments on your postings. Participation creates a feeling of belonging and motivates more communication.

- **Engage in Industry Conversations:** Join popular debates, take part in Twitter chats, and add to topics in LinkedIn groups. Expanding your network can also be achieved by leaving insightful comments on other people's work.

Work with Peers:
- Partnerships, including collaborative webinars or guest blogs, can help you reach new audiences. Working together with experts in your field broadens your audience to include like-minded people.

Make Use of Keywords and Hashtags

Making use of appropriate hashtags and keywords guarantees that the appropriate audience will find your material. Make sure to use pertinent hashtags in your LinkedIn and Twitter posts, as well as while participating in GitHub discussions.

Hashtag Strategies:
- Make use of both general and specific hashtags. While specialty hashtags like #PythonTips and #MachineLearning101 guarantee that you reach people who are particularly interested in your industry, broad hashtags like #tech and #developers help you reach a wider audience.

Assess and Modify

By monitoring your social media numbers, you may determine what kinds of material appeal to your audience and modify your approach accordingly. Tools that offer useful information on demographics, reach, and interaction include Google Analytics, LinkedIn Analytics, and Twitter Insights.

The engagement rate (likes, comments, and shares) is one of the key metrics to keep an eye on.
- Growth in followers
- Click-through rates (for links to blogs, articles, etc.)
- Demographics of the audience (area, sector, occupation)

You can improve your strategy and make sure you're providing the kind of material that your audience values most by routinely examining these indicators.

6.3. Using GitHub, Twitter, and LinkedIn to Manage Your Personal Brand

The art of influencing how others view you as a professional is known as personal branding. Across all of your social media accounts, you can project a consistent image that communicates your knowledge, principles, and personality by maintaining your personal brand. The three main platforms—LinkedIn, Twitter, and GitHub—that are the subject of the ensuing subsections are all essential to developing your personal brand in the tech sector.

Professional Portfolio on LinkedIn

The most significant medium for professional personal branding is LinkedIn. Your LinkedIn profile functions as a professional statement, portfolio, and online resume for developers, designers, and data scientists. Creating a thorough, well-designed profile that accurately represents your experience and career path is your aim.

Optimize Your Profile:
- A professional headshot, an attention-grabbing headline, and a well-written summary are all essential components of a full and current LinkedIn profile.

Headline: Be clear about your role and area of experience (e.g., "Data Scientist | Machine Learning Enthusiast | Python Expert") and include pertinent keywords.

- **Summary**: A story of your career aspirations, major accomplishments, and professional experience should be included in the summary section. Be succinct but powerful.

Exhibit Articles and Projects:

- Use the "Featured" section to highlight your major achievements, completed projects, and authored articles. This establishes you as a thinking leader and gives your profile more depth.

Take Part Through Thought Leadership:

- Write articles, offer opinions, or provide updates on the most recent developments in the field. Your visibility is increased when you regularly interact with your network by providing insightful material.

Twitter: The Instantaneous Link

Professionals and thought leaders converse in real time on Twitter, which makes it a great place to develop your personal brand. The capacity to communicate with people, take part in conversations, and provide brief, easily assimilated ideas is a major factor in Twitter success.

Write an Influential Bio:

- Your role, areas of experience, and interests should all be included in your bio. It's one of the first things people see, so make sure it's impactful and succinct.

- **Engage in popular Topics:** Stay up to date by tweeting live at conferences or participating in popular industry topics. This keeps you abreast of advancements in the business and expands your reach.

Make Threads on Twitter:

- Twitter threads are a useful tool for sharing a thorough analysis of a subject or offering in-depth thoughts. With this method, you are not constrained by the character count and can delve further into technical or industry-related topics.

GitHub: The Workplace for Professionals

For developers, GitHub functions as an interactive portfolio that highlights their abilities and project contributions. It's crucial for tech workers to keep up an active GitHub presence by sharing personal projects, participating in the developer community, and contributing to open-source projects.

Make sure your GitHub profile is comprehensive, including links to your personal projects, repositories, and any contributions you have made to open-source communities.

Continually Contribute Code:
- Consistently uploading code to GitHub shows that you are involved and actively involved in the development community. Regular engagement, whether in the form of group projects or personal endeavors, shows your commitment.

- **Participate in Open-Source Initiatives:** Contributions to open-source projects are a fantastic way to work with other developers and demonstrate your coding prowess. It's also a chance to become well-known in the development community.

Developing a great social media presence involves more than just gaining followers; it also entails fostering meaningful interaction and presenting your knowledge in an intelligent and professional way. You may establish yourself as a respected and valued expert in your field by selecting the appropriate platforms, using astute audience growth tactics, and maintaining your personal brand on GitHub, LinkedIn, and Twitter. Keep in mind that your personal brand is reflected in your online presence; treat it with respect and regularity.

CHAPTER 7

ESTABLISHING PROFESSIONAL CONNECTIONS AND NETWORKING

In the world of technology, networking is a crucial component of professional progress. Establishing a strong network of colleagues, mentors, and business executives can help developers find new possibilities, promote teamwork, and strengthen their personal brands. This chapter will examine the many aspects of networking in the developer community, such as its effectiveness, the benefits of going to industry conferences and meetings, and the significance of working together with other developers.

7.1. The Developer Community's Use of Networking

Making genuine contacts that can result in knowledge exchange, job progress, and mutual support is the goal of networking, which goes beyond simply trading business cards. Networking is essential in the developer community for a number of reasons:

- **Access to prospects:** Developers can access a wide range of employment prospects through networking. Having a network of connections who can speak out for you is essential because many jobs are filled through recommendations rather than standard job listings.

- **Exchange of Knowledge:** Interaction with colleagues and business executives promotes a culture of lifelong learning. Developers can greatly improve their abilities by exchanging ideas on emerging technologies, best practices, and project management techniques.

- **Guiding:** Developing connections within the developer community frequently results in chances for mentoring. A mentor can help you make important career decisions, connect you with powerful people, and offer priceless advice.

- **Innovation and Collaboration:** Through

collaborative ventures or open-source contributions, networking might generate ideas for project collaboration. Working together may create a sense of community and inspire creative ideas.

- **Maintaining Current:** The tech sector is changing quickly. Through networking, developers may stay up to date on the newest tools, technologies, and trends, which keeps them competitive and relevant in their industry.

Developers should use a few tactics to properly utilize networking's power:

- **Be Genuine:** Put more emphasis on developing genuine connections than on transactional exchanges. Take a sincere interest in the work and experiences of others.

- **Participate in Social Media:** To network with other developers, use sites like GitHub, LinkedIn, and Twitter. To build your visibility, share your projects, participate in conversations, and offer insightful commentary.

- **Follow Up:** Send a message or connection request once you've met someone, whether in person or virtually. Even a brief email thanking them for the talk might make a big difference.

7.2. Participating in Industry Gatherings and Conferences

Developers have an unmatched opportunity to network, learn, and develop at industry conferences and meetups. These gatherings provide forums for networking, professional growth, and knowledge sharing. There are several advantages to attending such events:

- **Acquiring Knowledge from Professionals:** Keynote speakers and workshops led by professionals in the field are common at conferences. Participants can learn about cutting-edge procedures, case studies, and new trends that can help them in their profession.

- **Networking Opportunities:** Events frequently have breakout groups, networking sessions, and casual get-togethers that promote conversation among attendees. These environments encourage dialogue that may result in beneficial alliances and teamwork.

- **Practical Workshops:** Numerous conferences have interactive workshops that allow attendees to learn new skills or experiment with cutting-edge technologies. Participating in hands-on activities can strengthen knowledge and promote teamwork.

- **Highlighting Projects:** Conferences give developers the chance to showcase their work, whether through poster sessions or speaking engagements, in an effort to establish their brand. This exposure might improve one's reputation and lead to new chances.

- **Comprehending market trends**: Developers can assess market trends and new technology by attending conferences. By knowing the direction the sector is taking, they may strategically position themselves for employment in the future.

Developers should think about the following tactics to get the most out of conferences and meetups:

- **Get Ready in Advance:** Examine the speakers, attendees, and agenda. Make a list of the people you want to connect with and decide which important sessions to attend.

- **Be Receptive to Discussions:** Be open-minded when you approach networking possibilities. Talk with guests who have different experiences and backgrounds. A casual discussion can go in many directions.

- **Engage in Active Participation:** Don't be a passive participant; give your thoughts, ask questions, and add to conversations. Making relationships and standing out can be achieved through active engagement.

- **Follow Up After the Event:** Get in touch with the people you met at the conference. Express gratitude for the chat and offer suggestions for future communication in individualized notes.

7.3. Working Together with Other Programmers

The foundation of the developer community is collaboration. Collaborating with others promotes creativity and originality in addition to improving technical proficiency. There are many advantages to working together:

- **Different Views:** Working together with people who have different experiences and backgrounds results in a variety of perspectives that can improve creativity and problem-solving.

- **The development of skills:** Collaborating with fellow developers facilitates the sharing of abilities and expertise. More seasoned colleagues can teach less experienced engineers, and newcomers can provide veteran devs with new perspectives.

- **Accountability and Motivation:** Accountability is

fostered via collaboration. Due to shared accountability, team members are more likely to maintain motivation and accomplish deadlines.

- **Creating a Portfolio:** Opportunities to collaborate on significant, high-caliber projects that can improve your portfolio are presented by collaborative initiatives. Employers may find it appealing to see examples of effective cooperation and teamwork.

- **Networking Possibilities:** Expanded networks are frequently the result of collaborative projects. Collaborating with others fosters new relationships and could lead to future partnerships or employment opportunities.

Take into account the following tactics to work with other developers more successfully:

- **Select the Correct initiatives:** Seek out initiatives that complement your abilities and interests. Select partnerships that offer chances for development and education.

- **Make Use of Internet Platforms:** Join cooperative coding clubs or look for open-source projects using websites like GitHub. These tools make project management, version control, and collaboration easier.

- **Express Yourself Clearly:** Successful teamwork requires effective communication. To keep organized and make sure everyone is in agreement, use communication systems like Slack or Discord and project management tools like Trello or Asana.

- **Accepting feedback is important.** Feedback is given and received as part of collaboration. Be receptive to helpful criticism and take advantage of the chance to grow.

- **Celebrate Successes Together:** Acknowledging and applauding accomplishments, no matter how minor, promotes a constructive team atmosphere and fortifies bonds.

Success in the developer community is mostly dependent on networking and establishing business connections. You may build a thriving professional ecosystem that encourages development, innovation, and opportunity by utilizing networking, regularly attending industry events, and engaging with other developers. Keep in mind that the connections you make today can influence your professional path future; make smart investments and enjoy the benefits.

CHAPTER 8

PARTICIPATING IN COMMUNITY AND OPEN-SOURCE INITIATIVES

Contributing to open-source and community projects gives developers a special chance to improve their abilities, expand their professional networks, and make significant contributions to the tech community in a time when teamwork and community-driven development are crucial. This chapter explores the advantages of contributing to open-source projects, how to choose projects that interest you, and efficient methods for showcasing your open-source work.

8.1. Advantages of Contributions to Open-Source

There are many advantages to working on open-source projects, which makes it a worthwhile experience for developers of all skill levels. Here are a few main benefits:

- **The development of skills:** Developers can use a range of tools, technologies, and coding techniques when they contribute to open-source projects. Gaining practical experience is crucial for improving technical proficiency, picking up new programming languages, and becoming an expert in development frameworks.

- **Practical Experience:** Contributions to open-source projects expose users to actual software development procedures. Developers gain knowledge of code reviews, project management techniques, communication workflows, and version control systems (such as Git), all of which are critical in work settings.

- **Networking Possibilities:** You may greatly increase the size of your professional network by participating in open-source groups. Developers can establish connections with maintainers, contributors, and business leaders, which may result in joint ventures and employment prospects.

- **Portfolio Enhancement:** Taking an active position in open-source initiatives gives your portfolio and resume more legitimacy. Contributions reflect initiative, a dedication to lifelong learning, and the capacity for teamwork—all qualities that prospective employers value.

- **Contributing to the Community:** One approach to give back to the IT community that has helped many developers over their careers is to contribute to open-source projects. This selfless quality promotes a feeling of direction and inclusion in the community.

- **Recognition and Visibility:** Community recognition can result from regular donations to high-impact projects. As developers gain recognition, they can be asked to publish articles, give talks at conferences, or assume project leadership positions.

- **Remaining Current**: As the open-source ecosystem changes quickly, developers who take part in these projects stay up to date on the newest trends, best practices, and technologies, which helps them stay competitive in the employment market.

Developers should approach projects with a growth attitude, seeing problems as chances for education and career advancement, in order to optimize the advantages of open-source contributions.

8.2. Locating Initiatives to Participate in

It can be difficult to choose one of the many open-source projects to donate to. Nonetheless, a few tactics can aid in expediting the procedure:

- **Determine Your Interests:** To begin, determine your areas of interest, be they data science, web development, mobile applications, or another discipline. You can identify initiatives that align with your interests and experience by focusing more narrowly.

Examine Well-Known Platforms: Numerous sites facilitate the discovery of opportunities and host open-source projects:

- **GitHub:** The biggest open-source project repository, GitHub provides tools to search repositories by topic, programming language, and other criteria. You can also look through popular repositories and "good first issue" issues to locate contributions that are appropriate for beginners.
- **GitLab:** Like GitHub, GitLab has a large number of open-source projects and an easy-to-use interface for finding and participating in projects.
- **Bitbucket**: Bitbucket hosts a range of collaborative projects and provides a community for contributors, while being less well-known for open-source projects than GitHub.

See Also: Open-Source Communities Finding projects and making connections with developers who share your interests might be facilitated by participating in committed open-source communities:

- **Open Source References:** These resources provide links to well-known projects seeking contributors as well as instructions on how to contribute to open-source projects.

The Mozilla Developer Network (MDN) is as follows: With an emphasis on web technologies, this platform provides a wealth of chances for contributors to enhance documentation and create new features.

- **FreeCodeCamp:** This foundation promotes a feeling of community and common purpose by inviting developers to participate in its coding projects and courses.

Take part in coding events and hackathons: Open-source projects that participants can contribute to are frequently a staple of hackathons and coding contests. Many projects actively seek contributors, and these gatherings provide a collaborative environment.

Follow Important Organizations and Developers: Pay attention to forums, blogs, and social media where prominent developers and organizations post information about their projects. Following them may lead to the discovery of new projects that require funding.

Participate in Developer Groups and Forums: Participate in interest-related online forums like Stack

Overflow, Reddit, or Discord communities. Developers encourage contributions and frequently share their open-source projects.

Examining the project's documentation, contribution policies, and community culture is crucial when investigating projects. Selecting a project that is in line with your interests and values will improve the experience and encourage a long-term commitment.

8.3. Presenting Your Work in Open Source

Presenting your open-source contributions in an effective manner can boost your professional reputation and lead to new chances. The following techniques will help you showcase your work:

Keep an Extensive Portfolio: Compile all of your open-source contributions into a portfolio. Describe the impact of your work on the project, highlight your specific contributions (such as bug fixes, feature additions, or documentation updates), and include links to repositories.

Make Use of GitHub Profiles: The focal point of your open-source work is your GitHub profile. Make sure it is comprehensive and adequately highlights your contributions:

- Repositories that showcase your finest work should be pinned.
- Compose succinct and understandable README files that outline the goals of each project, setup instructions, and ways that others can help.
- Provide details on the technology you employed, the difficulties you encountered, and the fixes you came up with.

Compose technical blogs: You can demonstrate your knowledge and perspectives by blogging about your open-source experiences. Post in-depth essays on your contributions to certain projects, the difficulties you faced, and the solutions you came up with. In addition to showcasing your abilities, this establishes you as a community thought leader.

- **Participate in Social Media:** Post your open-source work on social media sites like Twitter and

LinkedIn. To get more exposure, include pertinent hashtags. You should also think about producing posts that highlight your experiences, new abilities, or insights on projects you've worked on.

- **Make Your Own Website:** A personal website can be used as a CV, blog, and portfolio. Add sections that highlight your work on open-source projects, blog entries, and other pertinent experiences. Make sure it is both aesthetically pleasing and simple to use.

- **Get involved in conferences:** Think about offering to speak at conferences or meetings if you've contributed significantly to a project. You can make new contacts and raise your profile in the development community by sharing your experiences.

- **Emphasize Cooperation:** If working with others was a component of your efforts, recognize and honor those collaborations. This not only demonstrates your interpersonal skills but also supports the sense of community that is important to open-source development.

One of the most effective ways to advance professionally in the tech sector is to contribute to open-source and community projects. You may develop your abilities, create a solid professional network, and positively influence the community by realizing the advantages of open-source contributions, actively looking for projects that meet your interests, and skillfully presenting your work. In addition to promoting individual growth, the open-source contribution journey aims to promote cooperation and creativity among developers.

CHAPTER 9

ESTABLISHING YOURSELF AS AN AUTHORITY IN YOUR FIELD

For developers, becoming a thought leader is a huge advantage in the rapidly evolving technical landscape of today. Establishing oneself as an authority in your subject, influencing colleagues, and participating in the continuous discussion within the industry are all components of thought leadership. This chapter examines practical methods for building your credibility, improving your public speaking abilities, and producing technical articles and white papers that have an impact.

9.1. Establishing Your Authority

Understanding the specifics of your industry and the larger environment in which it functions is the first step towards establishing oneself as an authority in it. The following are some essential tactics for proving your authority:

Find Your Niche: Choose the particular area of your profession in which you have expertise and a strong interest. You can distinguish yourself and establish yourself as an authority by specializing in a particular field. This could include cloud architecture, web accessibility guidelines, or machine learning methods.

Create a Powerful Personal Brand: Your industry reputation is your own brand. Make sure it appropriately conveys your beliefs, abilities, and experience. This comprises:

- **Consistent Messaging:** Make sure that your messaging is consistent across all channels, including professional networks, personal websites, and social media.
- **Identity Visual:** Think about coming up with a unique visual theme or logo that embodies your business and using it consistently throughout your web presence.
- **Professional Internet Personas:** Make the most of your LinkedIn page and other professional sites by providing a thorough summary of your abilities, successes, and experiences. This becomes the basis

of your authority.

The tech industry is always changing, so it's important to stay up to date on the newest trends and innovations. Invest time on a regular basis in:

- **Online Courses and Certifications:** To stay up to date with industry advancements, pursue ongoing education via online resources such as Coursera, Udacity, or edX.
- Attend webinars and workshops pertaining to the sector in order to network with peers and gain knowledge.

Share Your Knowledge: You can greatly increase your credibility by sharing your knowledge and experiences.

- **Produce Instructional Materials:** Create content for your audience by hosting podcasts, creating videos, or writing blog entries.
- **Guide Others:** By mentoring less seasoned developers, you can strengthen your authority and foster goodwill in the community.

Connect with Other Professionals: Be in the company of

other influential people and professionals in your field. Participate in online forums, go to conferences, and have conversations that promote cooperation and learning from one another. Developing connections with other leaders can increase your reputation and visibility.

9.2 Presentations and Public Speaking at Events

Speaking in front of an audience is a great way to influence people and develop authority. The following techniques will help you become a more successful public speaker:

Build Your Speaking Ability: Make an investment in acquiring effective public speaking abilities. Examine the following strategies:
- **Join Public Speaking Organizations:** Groups such as Toastmasters International offer a helpful setting for honing your speaking skills.
- **Enroll in Speaking classes:** Examine workshops or online classes that concentrate on storytelling, public speaking, and presentation abilities.

Select Relevant Topics: Pick subjects that are both in line with your area of expertise and appeal to your audience. Possible areas of attention include:

- **Emerging Technologies:** Talk about cutting-edge technologies like blockchain, quantum computing, and artificial intelligence.
- **Best Practices:** Discuss best practices in project management, software development, and user experience design.

Create Engaging Presentations: When creating presentations, try to make slides that are both aesthetically pleasing and educational:

- **Use Visual Aids:** To highlight important ideas and maintain audience interest, use infographics, charts, and pictures.
- Incorporate storylines into your presentations by practicing storytelling. Anecdotes, case studies, or personal tales can help make abstract ideas more memorable and accessible.

Seek Speaking Opportunities: Make a concerted effort to speak at industry events, conferences, and meetups:

- **Submit Proposals:** Look into forthcoming events

and offer to speak. Make sure your proposal emphasizes the importance and pertinence of your subject.
- In order to exchange ideas and communicate with other professionals in real time, take part in panel discussions.

Involve Your Audience: Encourage audience participation in your presentations by incorporating interactive elements:
- In order to promote audience engagement and meet their interests, allot time for questions during Q&A sessions.
- **Live Polls:** Make the presentation more interactive by using live polling technologies to test audience knowledge or get their thoughts.

Get Feedback: To improve your abilities even further, get feedback following each presentation:
- **Ask for Constructive Criticism:** Invite audience members to share their thoughts on the topic, delivery, and style of your presentation.
- **Examine the video recordings:** Try recording your presentations and watching them again to see where

you may make improvements.

9.3. Composing White Papers and Technical Articles

Writing white papers and technical articles is a great way to demonstrate your knowledge and add to the conversation in your industry. Here are some tips for creating engaging content:

Select Related Subjects: Pick subjects that deal with issues, developments, or trends in the industry today. Think about:
- **Case Studies:** Give instances of actual projects you've worked on, emphasizing the achievements, difficulties, and lessons discovered.
- **Emerging Trends:** Write about new approaches or technology that may have an effect on your sector.

Do Extensive study: To guarantee that your content is precise and complete, do extensive study before to writing:
- **Use Credible Sources:** Cite credible journals, studies, and business reports to back up your assertions.

- **Remain Current:** To include the most recent information in your writing, keep up with advances and news in the sector.

Effectively Structure Your Content: Arrange your white papers or articles for readability and clarity:
- **Clear Introduction:** Begin with a succinct overview of the subject and its significance.
- To ensure a logical movement of ideas and to guide readers through the content, use headings and subheadings.
- Recap the main points and offer a call to action or suggestions for additional reading at the conclusion.

Involve Your Audience: Write in a way that appeals to your intended audience.
- **Use Plain terminology:** Steer clear of excessively technical or jargony terminology unless absolutely required. To reach a larger audience, strive for clarity.
- **Incorporate Visuals:** To visually represent difficult concepts and break up the prose, include charts, infographics, or diagrams.

Publicize and advertise your work: After writing your articles, think about where to publish them and how to market them.

- **Contribute to Industry Blogs:** Send in pieces to respectable tech blogs, online periodicals, or guest-posting websites such as Medium.
- **Share on Social networking:** To reach a larger audience, share your articles on Twitter, LinkedIn, and other social networking sites.

Interact with Your Readers: Promote reader participation by asking questions, leaving comments, or starting conversations:

- **Respond to Comments:** Encourage readers to interact with your content by answering their comments and starting conversations.
- Write follow-up articles based on reader comments or frequently asked questions.

It takes a dedication to lifelong study, clear communication, and community involvement to become a thought leader in your profession. You may greatly increase your impact and reputation in the tech sector by establishing yourself as an authority, improving your public speaking abilities, and creating top-notch technical content. As you set out on this path, keep in mind that thought leadership is about motivating others and advancing your area in addition to imparting knowledge.

CHAPTER 10

Keeping Your Personal Brand Strong and Developing It

Staying current in a rapidly expanding technical field as a developer requires upholding and developing your unique brand. Your personal brand should change and develop together with you as your abilities, experiences, and the industry as a whole do. This chapter looks at how to manage your reputation in the digital era, adjust your brand to new technologies, and put long-term plans for personal brand development into action.

10.1. Changing to Fit New Technologies with Your Brand

Maintaining your relevance in the ever changing world of technology necessitates taking the initiative to modify your personal brand to fit new tools and trends. Here are a few crucial tactics:

Remain Up to Date on Industry Trends: Any developer hoping to maintain brand alignment with modern technology must engage in ongoing learning:
- Get Industry Publications by Subscribing: To keep up with the most recent developments, read respectable tech blogs, journals, and publications on a regular basis.
- Keep up with thought leaders and influencers: Interact with content from prominent figures in the field on professional networks and social media sites. Their observations can yield important details regarding new technologies.

Invest in New Skills: Your skill set should advance along with technology.
- **Take Relevant Courses:** Take online classes, go to workshops, or take part in coding boot camps that concentrate on emerging programming languages or frameworks.
- **Take Part in Self-Directed Education:** To strengthen your flexibility, experiment independently with new tools and technologies using resources like

GitHub, Codecademy, or Coursera.

Update Your Online Presence: Make sure your online profiles reflect any new technologies or abilities you've acquired:

- **Revise Your Portfolio:** Update your portfolio frequently to include projects that demonstrate your proficiency with new technology or skills.
- **Update Your LinkedIn Profile and Resume:** Make sure your LinkedIn profile and resume appropriately showcase your most recent projects, achievements, and areas of experience.

Participate in Communities That Are Relevant: Participating in new technology-focused communities can help you become more credible:

- **Join Online Forums and Groups:** Take part in conversations on sites such as Reddit, Stack Overflow, or certain groups on Facebook or LinkedIn that are centered around technology.
- Participate in webinars and meetings: Participate in online or live events that highlight cutting-edge technologies related to your line of work. You can

share your views and learn from others by networking at these events.

Produce Content Concerning Emerging Technologies: Your brand can be strengthened by using content production to share your experiences with cutting-edge technologies:

- **Compose tutorials or blog entries:** Provide instructional materials that cover the new technologies you've embraced, along with best practices and advice.
- The creation of video content If you feel at ease in front of the camera, think about producing webinars or video lessons to showcase your skills.

10.2: Handling Online Reviews and Your Reputation

In the current digital era, your personal brand can be greatly impacted by your internet reputation. Maintaining a positive brand image requires actively monitoring your reputation and reacting to evaluations and feedback:

Keep an Eye on Your Online Presence: Continually see

what data is accessible online about you:

- **Set Up Google Alerts:** When your name appears in online debates or articles, Google Alerts will notify you so you may react quickly if needed.
- **Conduct Regular Audits:** To evaluate your online reputation, periodically look for your name on social media and search engines.

Participate in Feedback: Feedback, whether favorable or unfavorable, can offer insightful information:

- The way you reply to reviews Participate in online reviews on GitHub, LinkedIn, and other pertinent websites. Express gratitude to individuals who provide compliments and professionally respond to any criticism.
- Employing constructive criticism is important. Consider any unfavorable comments you get as a chance to improve. Take note of the issues brought up and think about how you may modify or enhance your strategy.

Preserve Professionalism Online: Your reputation is influenced by your online interactions:

- **Maintain Proper Digital Etiquette:** Even if you disagree with someone in an online discussion, be kind and helpful. Steer clear of contentious debates or unpleasant interactions.
- **Spread Good Content:** Post information that embodies your beliefs on a regular basis, such as accomplishments, industry insights, or useful resources for others.

Create a Positive Brand Story: Organize your web presence to convey a consistent and uplifting story:
- To highlight your career journey, regularly update your profiles with milestones, certificates, and accomplishments.
- **employ Personal Branding Elements:** To establish an identifiable presence across platforms, consistently employ brand components including logos, taglines, and visual themes.

Network Strategically: Developing connections with other experts will improve your standing:
- **Involve with Influencers:** Make connections with well-known individuals in your field to increase your

credibility by association.
- **Attend Networking Events:** Take part in industry events and conferences to network with colleagues and exchange ideas, enhancing your standing as an informed professional.

10.3. Long-Term Methods for Developing Your Personal Brand

To maintain its growth and relevance, a successful personal brand necessitates constant work and strategic planning. Here are some long-term tactics to think about:

Create Specific Objectives: Establish your personal branding goals and evaluate your success on a regular basis:
- **Determine Important Milestones:** Establish quantifiable objectives for your brand, such as attending a specified amount of networking events or producing a specific number of articles each year.
- **Review and Modify:** Review your objectives and plans on a regular basis, adjusting as needed in light of your development and industry shifts.

Diversify Your Content: You may reach a wider audience by producing a wider range of content:
- **Examine Various Media:** To keep your audience interested, think about experimenting with webinars, podcasts, or even interactive materials like infographics or quizzes.
- **Work Together:** Collaborate with other developers or professionals in the field to jointly produce material, incorporating a range of viewpoints and possibly expanding your audience.

Invest in Personal Development: Constant personal development is essential to the evolution of a brand:
- Participate in Professional Development Workshops: To improve your overall effectiveness, attend workshops on leadership, communication, and personal branding on a regular basis.
- **Seek Mentorship:** Make connections with mentors who can offer direction, criticism, and encouragement as you progress in your profession.

Build a Community: Creating a community around your brand can increase its impact:

- **Start a Newsletter:** Launch a newsletter in which you provide your audience with updates, articles, and insights. This may aid in building a devoted fan base.
- **Conduct Webinars or Gatherings:** Plan events, either in person or online, to engage your audience and impart knowledge, solidifying your position as a thought leader.

Continually Assess Trends: Maintain flexibility by routinely evaluating market trends:

- **Be Open to Change:** Be prepared to adjust your brand strategy in reaction to emerging technology or changes in the preferences of your target audience.
- Encourage a growth mindset by accepting setbacks and seeing them as chances for improvement.

As a developer, maintaining and developing your personal brand is an ongoing process that requires focus and work. You can make sure that your brand stays relevant and powerful in the rapidly changing tech scene by adjusting to new technologies, controlling your online reputation, and putting long-term growth strategies into place. In the end, a strong personal brand can help you become a leader in your industry, improve your professional reputation, and open doors to new prospects.

ABOUT THE AUTHOR

 Author and thought leader in the IT field Taylor Royce is well known. He has a two-decade career and is an expert at tech trend analysis and forecasting, which enables a wide audience to understand complicated concepts.

Royce's considerable involvement in the IT industry stemmed from his passion with technology, which he developed during his computer science studies. He has extensive knowledge of the industry because of his experience in both software development and strategic consulting.

Known for his research and lucidity, he has written multiple best-selling books and contributed to esteemed tech periodicals. Translations of Royce's books throughout the world demonstrate his impact.

Royce is a well-known authority on emerging technologies and their effects on society, frequently requested as a speaker at international conferences and as a guest on tech podcasts. He promotes the development of ethical technology, emphasizing problems like data privacy and the digital divide.

In addition, with a focus on sustainable industry growth, Royce mentors upcoming tech experts and supports IT education projects. Taylor Royce is well known for his ability to combine analytical thinking with technical know-how. He sees a time when technology will ethically benefit humanity.

www.ingramcontent.com/pod-product-compliance
Lightning Source LLC
Chambersburg PA
CBHW071058240526
45471CB00016B/1992